Coming Back to the Body

Coming Back to the Body

Poems

by Joyce Sutphen

Holy Cow! Press • Duluth, Minnesota • 2000

We gratefully acknowledge the careful editorial
attention given these poems by Connie Wanek.

The author also thanks the Minnesota State Arts Board for the Fellowship in
Poetry that supported work on this manuscript, as well as for a grant that will
allow for the reading of these poems in towns across Minnesota.
Thanks is also due the Jerome Foundation for the Study and Travel grant,
and to the Harmony Women's Fund for a residency at Norcroft Retreat on
Lake Superior. Special thanks to the author's colleagues at Gustavus
Adolphus College, who have always been encouraging and supportive.

This project is supported, in part, by a grant from the Arrowhead Regional
Arts Council through an appropriation from the Minnesota State Legislature,
and by generous individuals.

Library of Congress Cataloging-in-Publication Data
Sutphen, Joyce.
Coming back to the body : poems / by Joyce Sutphen.
p.cm.
ISBN 0-930100-98-0
1. Farm life—Poetry. 2. Minnesota—Poetry. I. Title.
PS3569.U857 C66 2000
811'.54—dc21   00-059810

Holy Cow! Press books are distributed to the trade
by Consortium Book Sales & Distribution (Saint Paul, Minnesota).
For personal orders, catalogs or other information, please write to:

Holy Cow! Press
Post Office Box 3170
Mount Royal Station
Duluth, Minnesota 55803

For Betty

Contents

I

Homesteading   11
In the Beginning   12
Comforts of the Sun   13
Here Is My Father   14
Fieldwork   15
Girl on a Tractor   16
My Father's Woods   17
The Shop   18
Semi-Literate   19
The Rosary of the World   20
A Poem with My Mother in It   21
Apple Season   23
Song, In Cut Time   25
Lost at Table   26
Fields in Late October   27

II

Casino   31
Of Virtue   32
Mending   33
The Silence Says   34
Doppler Effect   35
Resurrection #6   37
All Reason and No Rhyme   38
Wanted   41
A Kind of Villanelle   42
The Exorcism   43
Her Legendary Head   44
Perpetual Motion   45
The Word Behind the Word   46
Word Gets Out   47
Not for Burning   48
The Temptation to Invent   49

III

Sometimes Never   53
A Way to Survive   54
Condition   55
Natural Selection   56
The Seed   57
In a New Key   58

Bell Bottom Dream   59
How It Would Be   60
Not the Man   61
Possibilities   62
When She Tells Our Story   63
Launching into Space   64
Acoustic Alibi   65
Key of Dust   66
Will Come Again   67

IV
Bookmobile   71
Slowing Down the Globe   72
The Eiffel Tower   73
Chagall's Lovers   74
Rodin on Film   75
After Magritte   76
Arrangement in Grey and Black   78
On the Day You Leave Paris   79
On Hampstead Heath   80
Coram's Fields   82
Reading in the British Library   83
The Haircut   84
Trains   85
Highgate   86
Negative Capability   88
At Lissadel   89
Another Room   90
Night and Day   91

V
Late in the Century   95
What the Heart Cannot Forget   96
Waking Up as I Fall Asleep   97
Older, Younger, Both   98
Mimetic   99
The Only Name We Know   100
Photosynthesis   101
Gifted   102
Coming Back to the Body   103
Seeing off the Dead   104
Into Thin Air   105
The Assumption   106

Acknowledgements   109

I

Homesteading

Long ago, I settled on this piece of mind,
clearing a spot for memory, making a
road so that the future could come and go,
building a house of possibility.

I came across the prairie with only
my wagonload of words, fragile stories
packed in sawdust. I had to learn how
to press a thought like seed into the ground;

I had to learn to speak with a hammer,
how to hit the nail straight on. When
I took up the reins behind the plow,
I felt the land, threading through me,
stitching me into place.

In the Beginning

I think this place was often a village,
and smoke from the fires hung like
ropes in the air. I think we are standing
on bones and feathers, broken shells.

This place was star-crossed, moon
beamed, earth-quaked. The wind
blew on a silver horn, and light
went around in a golden bowl.

This place was once a river,
and before that it was a garden
filled with every kind of fruit tree,
everything that is good to eat.

I think something happened here;
I think this is the place where
deals were made, and angels held
their breaths in the sky above.

Comforts of the Sun

To someone else these fields would be exotic:
the small rows of corn stretching straight
as lines of notebook paper, curving slightly over
the rise of a hill; the thick green

oatfields, which I could tell them would turn
into the flat gold of summer straw;
the curled alfalfa, slung like a jacket
over the shoulder of horizon.

To someone else, the small groves of trees
along the barbed-wire fence would look like
shrines to a distant god, little remnants
of woodland standing against the tilling hand.

Someone else would need to be told
that my footprints, in a hundred different
sizes, are etched under layers of gray
silt at the center of the farmyard,

that bits of my father's skin are plowed
into every acre. They would have
to be told how I know each tree,
each rock too heavy to lift.

Here Is My Father

Here is my father, ready to cut (or rake
or bale) hay. Here he is, about to chop
(or shred or pick) corn. And here he is
with the plow (or harrow, combine,
corn-planter, or grain-drill). He is easy
astride the backless seat of an old
tractor, his dark-jeaned legs bent to the
clutch and brake, clanking the starter
crank underfoot when he stops, leaps
down to hook up a wagon that will
carry hay to the feeders, stones to the
gravel pit, and sometimes his children,
who walk, arms outstretched for balance,
across the stages he pulls behind him.

Fieldwork

My father chose his words the way he
plowed a field: straight ahead from
one thought to another, rhyme
falling into rhyme behind the pull
a furrow makes, steady along
the progress of sounds turned over
each other, all the way to
the ending of the line.

He loved to look behind at what he made,
one hand on the throttle, the other
rubbing afternoon into his knee,
speaking dry stubble
into fresh loam, the exhaust
of his engine an ellipses overhead.

Girl on a Tractor

I knew the names of all the cows before
I knew my alphabet, but no matter the
subject, I had mastery of it, and when
it came time to help in the fields, I
learned to drive a tractor at just the right
speed, so that two men, walking
on either side of the moving wagon,
could each lift a bale, walk towards
the steadily arriving platform and
simultaneously hoist the hay onto
the rack, walk to the next bale, lift,
turn, and find me there, exactly where
I should be, my hand on the throttle,
carefully measuring out the pace.

My Father's Woods

I know whose woods these are: they are
my father's woods, and so, by some
unspoken law, they are mine. In winter,
my father takes the horses and sleigh
and plows through the snow, deep
into his woods. I can hear him there,
hidden behind the curtain of gray trunks,
roaring and biting into fallen trees
with his sharp saws. Everywhere,
if I could bear to look, I would see
pieces of something I loved, cut into
long cords and stacked into firewood.
In the clearing, dark smoke would hang
over fresh mounds of golden sawdust.

The Shop

There was a window
filtering the sunlight,
dusty as it came,

and boxes of nails,
long and dark,
tin-colored and squat,

boxes of silver bolts,
washers and screws,
tacks, inch-long staples.

The vice that could crush
a finger hung open jawed
on the edge of the workbench;

the welding mask tilted
its flat and mouthless face
towards the rafters.

The old harnesses hung
in the back corner, their
work-lathered leather

soft as the reins of memory,
guiding him through the tangle
of one year into another.

Semi–Literate

Once I had no sense of the alphabet's
Song, of its long train that wound along
The top of the chalkboard in the schoolroom.

I was anxious about little pairs of letters
That seemed to hold hands and go off into
The woods together: c and d; e and...

F (that's right!); h and i (hi!); j and k.
And then there was the caterpillar of
L-m-n-o-p. What could that be?

I was sure it meant something, something
Important, but I've never met one yet.
Q-r-s was curious, that was certain,

T-u-v I liked because it reminded
Me of a little cabin by a lake
Where waves crashed on rocks all night. W.

Was that only one letter? One piece
Of the alphabet? Or did it come apart
To make another u and v? X, oh

Yes—that one made sense, but Y didn't
Sound the way it looked, and when you asked
"Why?" that wasn't it, but Z was something

I could love: a little striped horse, gazing
Out the window, longing to go home.

The Rosary of the World

If my memory could be unlocked,
It would not be by taste, but by beads
Rubbed between the fingertips, each one
Announcing a sad or joyful mystery,
Prayers packed neatly in Roman stone.

It would all come back: the embossed
Vinyl of the kitchen chairs, the chrome leg
Where I saw the long reflection of a
Kneeling body. "The family that prays
Together, stays together," said my mother

And ordered us, the ring of her hopes,
Down to the kitchen floor, so that anyone
Gazing across the lawn into that window
Would have thought it empty, not suspecting
The murmur that swirled around the table,

Hearing instead, the call of a blackbird
In the fields beyond the yardlight, beyond
Even the fences marking out our pastures
And woods, beyond to where the stars
Like a family, circled around the world.

A Poem with My Mother in It

The problem is getting her into the poem
where she doesn't want to be anymore than
she wants to be in the photograph, hearing
her make that rueful threat (as she steps into
place) about broken cameras and ruined film.

Once she's in, the problem is keeping her
there, with her feet up, ankles above the
heart (doctor's orders). Picture her, hurrying
down a street with a string of kids behind her,
all of them running to keep up.

It's the late 50's and we've just spent
an eternity in the dentist's office.
The downtown stores blur by: Kresges,
J.C. Penney, Samson Shoes, Woolworth's.
Let's get this show on the road! she says.

The problem is knowing how to say this
without using what she taught us to avoid:
sentiment and gush, words too sweet to
digest. Now (sometimes) I can find a
Mother's Day card plain enough to please her:

One not edged with lace, not stacked with
rhyme. On the cover, there's a woman
in a garden where tomatoes ripen, eggplants
turn their purple shoulder to the sun, parsley
greens under the blue sky.

She walks into sweet corn so tall
that it swallows her up. Mom, I yell,
come out! I can't see you anymore.
Take it! she says. It'll be the best
picture of me you've ever seen.

Apple Season

The kitchen is sweet with the smell of apples,
big yellow pie apples, light in the hand,
their skins freckled, the stems knobby
and thick with bark, as if the tree
could not bear to let the apple go.
Baskets of apples circle the back door,
fill the porch, cover the kitchen table.

My mother and my grandmother are
running the apple brigade. My mother,
always better with machines, is standing
at the apple peeler; my grandmother,
more at home with a paring knife,
faces her across the breadboard.
My mother takes an apple in her hand,

She pushes it neatly onto the sharp
prong and turns the handle that turns
the apple that swivels the blade pressed
tight against the apple's side and peels
the skin away in long curling strips that
twist and fall to a bucket on the floor.
The apples, coming off the peeler,

Are winding staircases, little accordions,
slinky toys, jack-in-the-box fruit, until
my grandmother's paring knife goes slicing

through the rings and they become apple
pies, apple cakes, apple crisp. Soon
they will be married to butter and live with
cinnamon and sugar, happily ever after.

Song, In Cut Time

In the morning, the sky was a glow
that filled the room. From my bed
on the floor I could see bare branches
crossing the pale blue. I had dreamed
something I would not
let myself remember.

In the morning, certain things sorted
themselves out. I saw myself
skating down a canal, scarf wound
about my neck, hands clasped
behind my back. I was whistling
the theme to *Elvira Madegan*.

I have always taken pleasure in
the symmetry of intricate design,
executed under the dome
of my ear. I let my glance
hover on a windowsill,
then fly.

How fortunate that I was not
born and bred in a clock,
but have learned my rhythm
seasonally, that my heart opens
and closes as easily as
a plowed field.

Lost at Table

The weave in the green tablecloth
is open. Enter, it says, and I do,
sinking down into warp and woof,
snug in a tiny linen homestead, somewhere
east of candlestick and west of tapestry napkin.

And if my disappearance is noticed,
they have ways to bring me back again:
conversation will hover, like heat-detecting
helicopters over endless acres of cornfields
and find me sleeping between the rows

or walking aimlessly, singing my song
to turn a thousand ears from green to gold.

Fields in Late October

The fields have turned their backs
to the cooling sun. They have gathered
the yellow stubble of summer and taken it
under the hills for the mice to eat.

Do not tell me how this turning happened.
I know it was the plow with its sharp claw
that ripped away the ripened skin. I know
the tractor roared each furrow into being.

Still I know the fields have turned
away from greening and from gazing
hopefully at the promise of a fickle sky.
The fields are through with growing.

It no longer matters to them what clouds
gather on the horizon, or what rain
is suspended over them like love,
something that never falls until too late.

The fields are sleeping. Do not disturb them.
Move quietly about your wintry business.

II

Casino

My mind is shuffling its deck tonight,
slipping one card over another,
letting them fall together at the corners;
the random hand of memory
is dealing from the bottom of the pack.

First: a bearded man emptying
the dragon kiln, then a woman
whistling, her face turned away
as she opens the oven. Next:
a big cat, six toes on each paw,
climbing up the yardpole. Last:
a pair of workhorses circling a tree
until they grind themselves to dust.

There is no one home in the world
tonight. Everyone is out of range.
The cradles are empty, the boughs
broken down. Trees go helter-skelter
and the wheel is creaking on its shaft.
Hit me, I say to the dealer. Hit me again.

Of Virtue

Assuming a virtue
if I had it not, I assumed
that virtue would find me,
which it did, and found me lacking,
and lacking it, I had to assume
that my pretense at virtue
was over, that use would never
change the stamp of nature, that
nature would not be changed by
using virtue as a customary thing.

Custom, however, meant
little to me, consisting only
in that I never wanted to make
the same move twice. I was ruined
from the start, born under
the hottest August sky, the
shimmer of summer on the
horizon, the loosened link
between green and ripe,
waters inviting but forbidden,
dog days slipping the leash.

Mending

It is not as easy as I thought it would be,
not as hard as it was. I, who was
supposed to be him, came out me, and
she is that mystery yet unsolved.

Often I consider the clock and
slice the hours into pieces. I watch the
calendar turn, take wing, and fly
over the rooftop with something in its beak.

Other times, I stretch myself flat
and let the needle of thought go neatly
in and out, the shining foot holding
the fabric steady, stitching up an edge.

Another time, I pull at the thread,
wondering. My mother, when she was
the age that I am, was exactly as she
is now, but me, I am all unraveled.

Each year, I notice more the sound
the world is making, how voices are
folded into the wind, one door
slamming, another opening.

The Silence Says

The silence says use your eyes now.
A leaf is just a manifestation of green,
a leaf has its own geometry.
What is the theorem for basswood?
What is the maple leaf's proof?

The silence says the beating in your wrist
is the rhythm you are always listening for
in the tabor and drums, in a blues note bending.
What is the time signature of loneliness?
What is that syncopated joy?

The silence hints that it has more to say,
it wants to ask you out to dinner,
or spend the weekend with you.
It needs you, is pointing a finger
in your direction, hoping to be irresistible.

It says these things in other languages;
it hisses, fills up with static, and sometimes it
goes off the air, leaving a long trail of quiet,
clean as newly braided rope and useful for
what it pulls behind, what it ties together.

Doppler Effect

When I meet her, she tells me
that she is writing like crazy,
that she never stops.

Every time I see her,
she tells me this,
so I begin to look

For the lines around
her eyes; I wonder
if she hides poems

Under her tongue,
or if she chews them up
and swallows them down

And then spins out a web
in the video white
light of the moon.

Her clothes, I suspect,
are lined with words;
there are sentences

Sewn into her pockets,
metaphors up her sleeve,
rhymes braided into

Her long hair.
I think of her
as an ink well,

As a deep reservoir
of black that spreads
itself across the page.

I can see what she is
writing. I am listening
to hear the sound of it again.

Resurrection #6

This time he means to put me in my place,
though often his words have unraveled me.
Do not expect anyone to believe that story,
he says, though I don't suppose you made
it up. He believes me with the enthusiasm
of a lifelong skeptic, fingers deep in the
wound of proof. He is relieved to see that
I can still breathe, that my limbs move, though
slowly, so out of practice with the ground;
he listens as my tongue begins to find its way
into words again, stays just long enough to
tell himself the damage is unnoticeable, a
temporary death that will never be recorded,
the ashes of that other woman mixed into
my clay, her heart never missing a beat into
mine, the two of us cheating the grave in unison,
one forgiving, the other already forgetting.

All Reason and No Rhyme

It was because of the bowl and
the spoon, hidden, so that no one else
could use them, because he refused to
take part in the risk of domestic
commerce, with its investment of wax
and polish, the sudden loss when the milk
slipped from the hand to the kitchen
floor, the fluctuation of dust
and fingerprints, the excess of rind,
eggshells, and coffee-grounds, which
would have led, despite their cost,
to profit at the breakfast table:
silverware gleaming sunlight,
plates warmed in the oven, tall
glasses filled with the fragrance of
of oranges. We could have
feasted upon those mutual returns.

It was because he made me stand
on one foot, biting the corner
of my lip, rubbing my hair
between a thumb and finger, I spoke
and then hesitated; I began again.
Words fell down, the force of gravity
stronger than hope. Pebbles lifted
my heart gradually, so that
when it finally brimmed the edge,
I could no longer tell if it was love
or hate—only that the bitterness
was more than I could swallow.

For this reason, I could never be
part of him, could not bear
to say the words "my husband"
or tell what he did for a living,
who he worked for, where I met him.

Walking, I never wanted to say
"Let us go then, you and I,"
as I did with other men
or with my daughters.
His step was not mine;
I could not, would not,
match it, and mine
was never a possible pace,
so erratic and wandering
it seemed to him.

When we talked, I used words
that did not fit my mouth,
words so hard I could only
gnaw at their edges, words so small
I could not taste them.
I did not desire to be edified;
I did not love simplicity
as he said he did. It was because
I could not sit, with my hands
folded in my lap, head bowed,
listening to a church-front voice.
I could not swallow my tongue,
could not weed out thoughts
like nettles in the grainy field of faith.

It could have been that I
was born under a bad star,
lacking the emotional equivalent

of a sturdy compass. So I,
defective and deflecting his gaze,
found my heart's ease in a tangle
of roads and telephone wire.

Or it could have been atomic
mushrooms opening over my crib,
could have been voices radio-waving
through the air, old photographs
scattered everywhere, reflections
on an empty screen. It could have been
all of these, the whole world
breaking down, faltering to a halt.

Wanted

My heart went
into hiding when it
heard footsteps
following it, when
it saw how close
it was to slipping away.
Sometimes it hid
in the kitchen, where
I stood at the stove,
my face averted;
sometimes it stayed
behind the groceries
I brought in, everything
on the list crossed off,
or in the mileage books
he put in the cars.

Even now, I am not safe
in his country.
There are warrants out
for my arrest,
and "Wanted"
does not mean
he wants me.

A Kind of Villanelle

I will have been walking away:
no matter what direction I intended,
at that moment, I will have been walking

Away into the direction that you now say
I have always intended, no matter what my
intention was then, I will have been

Walking away, though it will not be clear
what it was that I was leaving or
even why, it seems that you will say

That always, I was walking away,
intending a direction that was not towards
you, but moving away with every step,

Or, even when I pretended to be walking
towards you, only making the place
for my feet to go backwards,

Away, where I will have been walking,
always away: intention and direction
unknown, but knowing you will always
say I will have been walking away.

The Exorcism

It was homemade and primitive,
like pulling a tooth with a string
and a slamming door, like taking out
an appendix by kerosene light
where dogs wandered in and out
the dirt-floored room.
Nothing for the pain that
everyone wanted to examine,
the twisted heart they thought
they could shout back into place.

Moaning and fluttering their fleshy hands
on the wind, on the wail of the soul possessed,
they certified her in a manner Inquisitional,
frantic when she held to the grip of darkness,
grimly determined to wait the thing out,
something learned from movie sheriffs,
white hats ghostly in the moonlight.

When she would not answer (though they
conjured her by heaven and by the all
mighty names they knew), they laid hands
on her and shouted down the well of her eyes.
Many tongues twisted in their mouths when
she went, leaving behind only
the smallest tooth of wickedness.

Her Legendary Head

This is the way the woman in
a Picasso painting feels, with her
mobile nose holding two eyes
to one side, her quivering lip
ascending into a pointed chin.

The world is now (and she
can hear its roar) all a blood-
dimmed tide, things fall
apart and then together, banged
and whimpering they begin.

All her life, she was up to
her neck in marble, and
the gyres in her head. Just
another woman in pieces,
inventory lost, instructions

too small to read. Broken
the lines of her, a memorially
reconstructed version, awaiting
the detection of each separate
and mysterious error.

Perpetual Motion

Since you left, I have gone back to believing
that the world is flat, that there be dragons.

Waiting in lonely stations, I count squares
in the ceiling, pretending I am brave.

Soon I stop noticing lovers the way I used to.
People turn away from each other while I watch.

I no longer see strangers who remind me of you;
they all look like someone I never knew.

Now there are no stars in the sky, no moon,
no ships on the horizon, no letters in the box.

This is what it is like: the rain starts coming down,
and pieces of my heart float by on the river everywhere.

The Word Behind the Word

This morning I can remember a word
that was lost last night, hidden behind
some other words: shy child, slipping
out of the photograph, leaving only the
shadow of a shoulder behind, unnoticeable
unless you knew she was there.

Lonestar. I said it and thought how
different it was from the word Texas,
which had smiled into my mouth
last night and made me think of
ten-gallon hats and steaks on a grill.

And how different also from Lodestar
or Star of the North: not guiding,
but lonely in its state of mind.

Word Gets Out

I write, despite the suspicion
that I can not leave this place,
not even in the disguise of ink,
and that my words will never
reach you as I intend, but smoke
their miserable way into the earth,
the unfavored offerings of a dark hour,
the memory of which will not rise,
but return in the gape of a window,
or the empty lot where weeds push
an old tire, and (always) the sidewalks,
crumbling and filled with wicked cracks.

If, somehow, this does reach you,
forgive the years when the senseless
war dragged on and supplies grew scarce.
Forgive me that I could not afford love,
its price gone far beyond my reach,
as I forgive you for thinking that
I surrendered and lost all hope.

Not for Burning

I come across your old letters,
the words still clinging to the page,
holding onto their places patiently,
with no intention of abandoning
the white spaces. They say
that you will always love me,
and reading them again, I almost
believe it, but I suspect that
they are heretics, that later,
in the fire, they will deny it all.

Then I remember something I once
read (my memory is filled with voices
of the dead): that it is a heretic which
makes the fire, and that I am more guilty
than your words, poor pilgrims who trusted
the road you sent them down and kept
severely to the way. I forgive them;
I let them live to proclaim freely what
they thought would always be true.

The Temptation to Invent

It is very strong,
especially when the memory is hazy.

It begins with "I once knew a man,"
and ends with "but it didn't work out."

I always remember something more substantial
than the details, something that does not translate.

Most of what I know is contagious. I
caught it from reading books and passed it on.

But tenderness has disappeared from my tongue;
parts of my heart are missing.

I realize that plot is not essential,
but I get tired of just words, words, words.

Reflecting is simply my way of turning away
from the past. What you see is no longer happening.

III

Sometimes Never

Talking, we begin to find the way into
our hearts, we who knew no words,
words being a rare commodity
in those countries we left behind.

Both refugees and similarly deprived,
we marvel at the many things there
are to say: so many variations
and colors of the same thought, so

many different lengths in the words
that line up together on our tongues.
No scarcity, no rationing, no
waiting in line in order to buy

the same answer we heard each time
we asked, that one word, owned by
the state, manufactured by the state,
serving all purposes equally alike:
No, No, No! . . . and sometimes, Never.

A Way to Survive

One night, in the middle of it, when
I could not sleep, I began to think
about failure and how to accomplish it:
how not to succeed in business without
really trying, how not to win
the lottery, how to take each
highly unrecommended step
as carelessly as possible, how
to lose friends and influence no one.

Then I thought: Perhaps I am working
too hard at missing the beat, perhaps
some unconscious, but calculating, Darwinian
sense is leading me, against my worst
judgment, into choosing the surest
way to survive, if nothing else.

Condition

They say that there is no evidence for evolution,
that the whole saga of gradual change
exists only in theory.
Perhaps, then, we should simply accept
this new creation in us and rest in it,
as on a seventh day.

This would give us more than an ocean
of chance, that against all odds, I,
in my unlikely sailing,
should come across you, who just happened
to be passing by, the one
perfect link.

Nothing so unlikely could be to my liking,
better that the fates decree or that some
hidden plan intervene.
So we might take heart, adjust gracefully to the miraculous.
So we might make another move, instinctively
trusting the way.

Natural Selection

How much there is we do not know
about each other: what is it I have not even
thought to tell you? memories that are
sealed away untouched as caves
in Southern France with their drawings of
animals that appear nowhere else, surprising
archeologists into remembering how much
they do not know about people who lived
in similar caves in similar terrain, under
identical moons and stars, a consistent expanse
of wind and rain, and even so harbored
a singular affection for the owl, the panther,
and hyena, though all their neighbors
loved only the bison and the bear.

The Seed

The same seed, sleeping in its granary,
is hard and tight and dry. It only moves
when the shovel dips into the bin,
and follows the flow that
fills the hollow in.

The same seed, sliding to the granary floor,
is lifted up and scooped into a sack.
It nestles in the gunny-cloth,
then rides the air
upon its back.

It slides in the seeder as it bumps its way
across the harrowed field, slipping
through the wooden sieve,
packed in earth,
and set to live.

The same seed, dreaming in the cold wet ground,
is loosened by the fingers made of rain.
It feels a cracking along its seam,
and becomes the force
of green again.

In a New Key

It was dissonant when it first
came to mind, but I knew that
gradually it would slip into the
coat that repetition wove.

I could see that this music
might please other ears, that
they might prefer it to the thing
I'd played so carefully.

This would say how my heart
went from its chair by the window
to the slamming door and on
to the quiet repairing.

It could hold onto the line of my thought,
hooked in its circling, ready to surface.
It listened until I was talking its language,
almost like a natural-born speaker.

Bell Bottom Dream

She steps off the curb
into the world that is
upside down like the
bottom of a puddle
where clouds glide
across the blue ice sky
and trees lean in
to get a closer look.

She never noticed
the tiny reflection her eyes
made in the mirror
or wondered at
the way a smile
is repeated, one
curve inside
another. She
had not paused
to consider
the way each link
on a chain twists
its way into another
but traveled on, never
thinking of the distance.

How It Would Be

This is how it would be:
you would come and
put your hands
on my shoulders.
The wind would lift
the curtains,
we'd hear leaves
on the road.

I'd look up from
my book,
reluctantly
at first.
The wind
would blow again,
harder this time.

A piece of paper
would go up
into the air,
then fall.

One of us
would close
the window,
the other would bend
for the paper, which
would be a poem,
like this one.

Not the Man

You are not the man I was looking for.
You arrived unexpectedly, like a letter
announcing that I had won some contest
I didn't remember entering,

telling me, in the most tasteful language
that I am now filthy rich, asking
do I want it all at once,
or in monthly payments?

I step back, in the doorway of my
modest expectations and say, over
and over, "Are you sure there's no mistake?"
wondering if I can afford this fortune.

And how will you tame my straydog heart,
used to roaming for a scrap of love?

Possibilities

What I mean to say is that I love oats
when they spill into the back of a pickup.
I watch corn stalks turning the light into silk.

That is why I go to the jack-in-the-pulpits,
trilliums, shelf mushrooms, bloodroots and violets.
I run the barefoot paths again, I find the deer track.

Among other pleasures, I have stood on hills
sailed over with blue and yellow, and I have
lived in treetops, birds always at my feet.

Cloud to ground, lightning to tree, the sky is
dropping its apron full of rain. Let me tell you
how the blue walks backwards in the wind.

When She Tells Our Story

It occurs to me, while she is telling, once again,
how we met, that she never tells a story
the same way twice, though the true part
at the center never changes.

We both know that we will come out better
when she describes us: we are her
Tristan and Isolde, Abelard and
Heloise. Always meant to be.

She always says how she met us together
and assumed we were. Each time she
explains, it is more clear that we were
the ones making the mistake.

She makes me remember something different
every time she tells it: us taking giant steps,
swinging a little girl between us, lifting her
up over the cracks in the sidewalk,

How you were the lights following me
home, the man walking away in my
mirror, a gaze that never lost
me, wherever I went.

Launching into Space

At a certain stage, the engine drops
into the ocean and thrust carries the capsule
onward into space, where it is not dark
and star-studded as everyone always imagines,
but light as Milton's celestial fields, and fiery.

At a certain stage, the caterpillar disappears
into the gauzy wrap of its spun cocoon, and
hangs like an unfurled leaf from the branch.
Inside, the neat machinery of wing and antenna
is unfolding, the slow loom weaving its color.

A child, at a certain stage, will develop a sense
of distance and continuity. Until then, she will
think that the ball rolling behind the chair has
vanished. She will not expect you to return.
Later, she will see through walls to where you are.

And love, at a certain stage, will know exactly
when to look across the room and smile, when
to turn and say the words it almost would not
say, like bringing in an armful of wood,
something to keep the fire against the cold.

Acoustic Alibi

I see from the diagrams that some sounds
stay in the voice's box and reverberate there,
even though the lips are parted, and the throat
is open. It appears that other sounds escape
to make their nests in the branches outside the
mouth, like water forced through a hose:
thin when the nozzle is twisted tight,
thick as rope when the channel clears, when
the sluice-gate is lifted, when the plug is pulled.

Is it an "a" or an "o"? What mark does
a vowel leave in the air? What tracks are made
by a herd of limping consonants, all of them
rubbing the places where they were chained
together, the broken fetters of words,
like the scattering of chaff as when the smooth bud
breaks into flower?
                          This is meaning's
acoustic alibi. It says that it was there
all the time and meant no harm. It says
it was going about its business and had
no intention of making itself into something
that would cheer the heart and nourish
the blood, but since you asked, it was
willing to pour itself out, perfectly willing
to become whatever you wanted to hear.

Key of Dust

Breathing in, I breathe the skin of trees,
the husk of rocky kernels cracking,
slagging off the shroud of centuries.

Into my lungs, a stream of atoms comes:
bits of Rome, bung-hole fillers—that
mighty Alexander, the scarce-bearded Caesar!

I am all that I am not, and I am not
what I shall become—who knows?
Not I, and the less I know

the further I fly, thistle-downed,
through golden-light unleafing, the grassy
blade, plucked up to make a crowing caw.

Breathing out, I breathe these latest words,
the cells of heart and lung in every vowel,
flittering pulse of inner ear,
trail of dust and ink.

Will Come Again

Every morning, as the year nears April,
I wake up with a dream that I carry
into the day: a fish in a creel,
out of its element.

I look out and see the trees are
dry gray against the clouds. By now
every bit of sap has drained back
into the ground. It begins to rain.

On the table, a vase of daffodils turns
its ten lion faces to the corners of the room.
The yellow is the color of maple leaves in
September. Thick stems whorl rootless in glass.

Nothing is immediately obvious. One day,
in a dream, the fish will swim through the air,
its fins bright-colored as a bird's wing.
Sap will rise, and the leaves will come again.

IV

Bookmobile

I spend part of my childhood waiting
for the Stearns County Bookmobile.
When it comes to town, it makes a
U-turn in front of the grade school and
glides into its place under the elms.

It is a natural wonder of late
afternoon. I try to imagine Dante,
William Faulkner, and Emily Dickinson
traveling down a double lane highway
together, country-western on the radio.

Even when it arrives, I have to wait.
The librarian is busy, getting out
the inky pad and the lined cards.
I pace back and forth in the line,
hungry for the fresh bread of the page,

Because I need something that will tell me
what I am; I want to catch a book,
clear as a one-way ticket, to Paris,
to London, to anywhere.

Slowing Down the Globe

I remember it spinning on its axis,
the continents blurred into blue
over the sound of a calliope.

Round as a softball it came, the twist
of the stitched seam floating
towards me,

the plate twirling on the stick,
first one, two, then
wild applause

from the crowd in the dark outside
of the center ring, each face
a planet,

their hands clapping the way stars do
when a careless muse
sings.

The Eiffel Tower

I walk under it,
looking up through
the brown iron lattice
(so light and spidery!)
at the sky, which now
billows blue between
the filigreed arches—
intricate!
stupendous!—
resting, they say,
on the banks of the
Seine with about
the same force as a
man, sitting in a chair.

Chagall's Lovers

All of his lovers are airborne.
They wear their wedding clothes
in the cornflower blue sky; they
embrace above rooftops,
above crimson trees.

Spoon to spoon, they fit together,
floating through the air with horses,
roosters, and flower bouquets.
Everything moves to
a fiddler's tune.

If they were angels, they would announce
their love in a blur of wings. Minstrels
and madmen adore them. They show
the sweet way to mystery,
even before you ask.

Rodin on Film

Rodin is at the top of the stairs
like a sculpted man. He stands still
until, on command, he comes down,
down, down, as if descending a throne.

Pygmalion-like, he is thinking of
flesh, of flesh turning to stone, stone
turning to bone, moment without
movement, marble into motion.

Rodin works his hammer and
chisel, blinks away stone with a
flickering eye, and steps back
(rough-flaked with marble)

to turn the torso on its wooden
pedestal, wedge his chisel, strike,
turn it again, and strike another
blow. He does these things for

the camera; he already knows how
it will work: how it will make his
body into flat dead air and then
let it pretend it is heavy with life.

After Magritte

A horse and rider move between the trees,
stepping gracefully through the wood.

In a photograph, the artist leans slightly
toward pieces of a woman held together

with Plexiglas. A locomotive is smoking
straight out of the fireplace.

The sky is raining men in bowler hats.
This is not a poem, it is an egg in a cage.

This is the canvas that fills the part
of the landscape missing behind it,

this is the silhouette of a vase holding up the light,
a pale blue afterglow edging the chimney,

the thin scar of a silver moon—there,
in the middle of his forehead. This is not

a poem, this is a leaf pretending to be a tree,
veins outstretched, green factories working overtime.

Here, lovers kiss through dark veils and
white cloth winds round the standing sleeper,

rifles bleed into the carpet and doors
open into night. I begin by putting pieces

into place, ready to make another pipe, another
poem: the same heart, different words.

Arrangement in Grey and Black

I wonder how the artist got
his mother to hold still
long enough for him to paint her.

Wasn't she constantly getting up
to bring him a cup of tea?
to find the brush he needed?

Didn't she tell him at least
a dozen times that no one would
want to look at an old woman?

At last, he turned her sideways
and told her to look out the window
while he painted her profile.

The sky was deepest blue,
and the clouds went over the horizon
like salmon, leaping up a golden stair.

"Oh Jimmy," she whispered, but
did not move, only her glance
brightening beneath the darkened brows.

On the Day You Leave Paris

On the day you leave Paris, the skies
are mostly cloudy, and the streets
are wet. Time flies
with a slow wing; it beats
its rhythm in nearly understood voices
in the hallway. If only we could speak
again of things that both of us desire:
instead of embers then, a fire.

In the evening, after reading
in the American Library, I fall asleep
and dream I see
as in a crystal ball
your airplane landing on a frozen lake,
your face sleek as an icicle, your beard
white as snow. I wake to say
I wish you would not go,

but words like these mean nothing
now, foreign bells that will not ring.

On Hampstead Heath

When I opened the book, bits of grass
fell out from the pages—pieces of
Hampstead Heath falling into the
William Morris willows of my bed.

It is lonely here on winter's shore
and hard to imagine those green
sociable hills and the two of us
on a park bench one June morning.

I was reading *Mrs. Dalloway* out
loud, and your head was resting
in my lap. All around us the air
was filled with winged seeds

that parachuted down from where
children were flying their kites into
the grove in which the Keats House
was not yet open to visitors. You

wanted me to see Kenwood House
so that you could impress me with
your knowledge of porticoes and
fluted columns, but we found

it difficult to navigate the park and
arrived hot and sweaty to gaze on
cool as cucumber Gainsborough women
and one ringletted girl by Vermeer.

Afterwards, you were disappointed
that I wasn't dazzled by the oblong
curve of the library ceiling, the triple
mirrors and book-lined apsidal ends.

But what's an apsidal compared to Keats's
chairs, pulled side by side so that he could
lean his head against his hand as he read?
What's better than a nightingale's garden?

Coram's Fields

I wake to the rooster's crow in Coram's Fields,
where only the children can go, with the gates
of Mecklenburgh Square just around the corner.

London is hushed, as in some engineless time.
The wind lifts the dark verge of the trees;
I hear the green rustle, watch a leaf fall.

Over in Russell Square, the man is opening
the café and tipping down the chairs. Already
someone wanders in to order cappuccino.

The sun is bright along Bedford Place. People
walk by slowly, glancing through the opened
doors, catching only a hint of lamp or drape.

Old men are playing tennis on the court,
and the sound of it goes back and forth
in my ear, conjuring with the wind.

I confess it was curiosity drew me here,
no intention of making you suffer.
I missed you—and London—of course.

Reading in the British Library

In the British Library, I forget the Elgin Marbles.
The Sphinx and the Lions of Amenophis
recede across the desert of the afternoon.

Away in the kingdom of ink, I can only use
a pencil. I go back to the Reading Room,
gold ribbons lifting the blue dome above me.

The scholar is discovered in his nap by two others.
They laugh and talk of home, oblivious
to the silent shade of the hour.

Later, the barrows rumble past as if they are about
to disappear into a dark shaft of thought;
old books fall softly onto one other.

Pages rustle and sigh, making me remember them
later when I walk through Russell Square
under leaves that whisper in the breeze.

The Haircut

On the edge of an ocean,
a star tears itself apart.
It anchors in the rock
with the tug of a foot,
and then, one ray walks away,
right angles to the rest.

In London, a woman leans
out the window and lets
hair from her brush float
into the night. Pieces
of her skin slip down
into the Thames.

His eyes are in the mirror
above hers. His smile is over
her smile; his eyebrows are
dark curves reflecting hers.
She is looking up
and into his face; he is
looking down into her gaze.

The scissors float all around
in the glass: at the corner of
her eye, just over her ear.
The sound of it is the clash
of swords, knives sharpening,
the steady sound of rain.

Trains

I missed you all those years, when
we would arrive at opposite sides
of the station, and your train would
blur you away, or mine would leave
you standing on the platform.

It was peaceful then, the two of us
sitting there: you, facing one way,
me the other, both of us reading
our paperback novels. I wanted to stay
there long enough to finish the book.

Where were you going then, if not
my way? I used to wonder. Once
you waved at me because your train
was late and mine was early. We sat
in our trains that almost touched,
waiting for them to pull us apart.

Highgate

In such a place, the aspect of death is softened.

Lady's Newspaper (1850)

You have to imagine the sunny slopes that Londoners
came to picnic on and how afterwards they might
stretch out full length, trying on a plot of ground for size.
You have to realize that you could see back across
to the Unreal City from this the real and final metropolis,
that Fleet Street and Cheyne Walk would give way to
Egyptian Avenue, the Circle of Lebanon, or some
nameless boulevard beyond the row of chestnut trees
planted to keep the nonconformists out of view.

And imagine the century passing. The menagerie owner dies
and leaves a sleeping lion on his tomb; the dog of the
barefisted fighter, chief mourner at his master's funeral,
lowers his huge head on his paws and keeps watch.
Faraday, as in life, keeps only to himself, dreaming
oceans of electricity: the great globe lit by his finger.
Rossetti, at home while the grave is opened by gaslight,
waits as the seals on the casket are broken and
the doctor extricates the manuscript from
Lizzie Siddal's red hair, grown so long it fills the coffin.

Then the land takes over; trees and bushes rise, their roots
overturn monuments: angels, beasts, harps, and horns.
The green grows and leaves everything in a ruined shade.
We walk, a little entourage of sightseers, passing
under the ceiling of trees, our eyes adjusting to the gloom,
discerning a marble wing here, a Celtic cross there.

Our guide does not tell us everything: he doesn't mention caskets rigged with bells and airpipes, in the unlucky event, and the bodies stolen from the mausoleum shelves, or vagrants slipping over the walls to sit on a tombstone drinking gin.

Our guide halts and talks, talks and walks. He knows everything there is to know about restoration. He knows about untwining ivy from a marble face, about blowing dust out of an ear. While he explains the tunnel that carried the coffins under the road, two men pass a joint back and forth, back and forth. A pair of lovers lean together and whisper; cameras click, pause, and click again: each a little burial of the moment, our faces shuttered, just as they are . . . now.

Negative Capability

—that is, being capable of being in
uncertainties, mysteries, doubts, without
any irritable reaching after fact and reason.
                    Keats, December 1817

I must conclude from this photograph
that I was standing above you on the hill,
taking no thought apparently for the
unflattering angle at which your gaze
would have to travel, toe to chin.
You seem content, even pleased
to look up at me, your left eyebrow
lifting slightly.
                    Was this picture taken
before or after we fell asleep on
the hillside and I had that dream about
rolling into the sea, which was in fact
crashing down below us?
                    Or was it after
I attempted a short cut through the bramble
faltering on the path of my own choosing?

Was it before late tea in St. Ives, where
we ate every crumb, every lick
of clotted cream and jam, tipping the pot
to get every drop? It was. Perhaps.

At Lissadel

We saw, from the gravel driveway, the great
windows, and, on that first visit, watched a
man and woman forage in a dumpster.

The clouds hung down over the dismal stone
as we circled the house in friendly talk.
I wondered how much of what we said

Was part of a past that we only knew
because the poet made it what it was
and spoke the words that we remembered now.

We know that beauty has an enemy,
but memory summons it back from time.
They were in silk kimonos, two girls, both

Beautiful. It was evening, and the light
came in the open windows; summer
was in the great green trees of Lissadel.

Inside the old Georgian mansion they talked
around the table; shadows on the wall
gathering like clouds before a storm.

Next came age and loneliness: beauty bleared
by desperate politics, the folly
of a hopeless cause and ignorant hearts.

Evening and another time: we circle
the gray bone of the past, speaking his speech,
never sure of what it is we know.

Another Room

Imagine the room: heavy furniture,
wooden shutters closed from inside.
Along the edges and between the slats,
the light of morning flares its blue
under-shadow, like a wing in flight.

The song in the radio is steamy, dark
as her coffee as she reaches over to turn
it up. The gulls are crying over the bay;
the tide is out. All the boats are leaning
on their sides like bright wooden toys.

She thinks of the sun coming over
the Irish Sea—like a rosary rubbed
through the gnarl of the cloudy sky—and
of her daughters: three small silhouettes
(heel and toe) dancing the soft tap of the shore.

Night and Day

The music on the radio
was made in Australia.
My dreams
were made in China.
Pieces of the globe
float in my head.
I am speaking in tongues;
I have the gift of prophecy.

Morning is here.
I drag my body up.
I set her on her feet.
She shuffles,
hesitates, looks back.
She forgets whatever she was!
She pretends to be human,
remembers the English words.

At evening, I wait
on my windowsill
horizon. My ship
sets out for the West.
I am air. I am fire.
The mother of beauty
is waiting, sleeplessly
to take me home.

v

Late in the Century

Sometimes my world slips
on its axis and words
lose their letters.
I say one name
and mean
another.

I know I will not always
return to you, nor will
you come back
to me. This is
the modern
world.

Knowing this, I drink
all the bright light
from a cup of
red hibiscus
opened this
morning.

Already there is darkening
in the leaves. Every
minute eats the next
with a ferocious
and delicate
appetite.

What the Heart Cannot Forget

Everything remembers something. The rock, its fiery bed,
cooling and fissuring into cracked pieces, the rub
of watery fingers along its edge.

The cloud remembers being elephant, camel, giraffe,
remembers being a veil over the face of the sun,
gathering itself together for the fall.

The turtle remembers the sea, sliding over and under
its belly, remembers legs like wings, escaping down
the sand under the beaks of savage birds.

The tree remembers the story of each ring, the years
of drought, the floods, the way things came
walking slowly towards it long ago.

And the skin remembers its scars, and the bone aches
where it was broken. The feet remember the dance,
and the arms remember lifting up the child.

The heart remembers everything it loved and gave away,
everything it lost and found again, and everyone
it loved, the heart cannot forget.

Waking Up as I Fall Asleep

I turn on the news to fall asleep,
but what I really want to know is
how my life is turning out.

I wonder if I could find myself
if I had to. How would I think in
that situation, I ask myself.

Where is the first place I would look
if I lost me? What kind of
disguise would I wear?

Would I look like her? Could she
talk like me? Does she have any
odd hobbies, I wonder, and

has she been spending money that I
don't have? Who does she talk to
when she wants to know

what I am thinking? Would I
listen? Why is it that when I am
talking to her I always think of

something to say after I've gone away?
When will I come back again, and
will she recognize herself when I walk in?

Older, Younger, Both

I feel older, younger, both
at once. Every time I win,
I lose. Every time I count,
I forget and must begin again.

I must begin again, and again I
must begin. Every time I lose,
I win and must begin again.

Everything I plan must wait, and
having to wait has made me old, and
the older I get, the more I wait, and everything
I'm waiting for has already been planned.

I feel sadder, wiser, neither
together. Everything is almost
true, and almost true is everywhere.
I feel sadder, wiser, neither at once.

I end in beginning, in ending I find
that beginning is the first thing to do.
I stop when I start, but my heart keeps on beating,
so I must go on starting in spite of the stopping.

I must stop my stopping and start to start—
I can end at the beginning or begin at the end.
I feel older, younger, both at once.

Mimetic

The sun (the moon, that bare bulb
hanging from the ceiling) gives light.
The bird (the butterfly, that airplane
winding up its engine) takes flight.

In all we do we replicate
all that is, was, and ever will be.
What most we love, most hate,
what we imagine is what we see.

The leaf turning color against the sky,
blackberries ripening on the stem,
skin wrinkling around the eye,
heart starting and stopping again.

Which is the form, which is the shadow?
Real or reflected, above or below?

The Only Name We Know

It's funny how a name takes hold
of the body, how the first thought
we had about someone persists.

We see a face across the room,
and right away we know that one
is going to change everything.

Even when we get to know them
better, when we realize they
weren't who we thought they were,

We keep thinking that they are that
other person, that name that came
to us the first time we met.

Photosynthesis

Morning falls out of its orbit
and swims up through the blue.
Last night, when I heard the news,
I forgot my human hunger.

Now I am making calculations
with a row of ivy and an old hibiscus.
I am silent as a shadow in the ferns,
I am frond green and curled.

It may be necessary to drink through
the roots; I could eat sunlight and air,
start a green factory in each finger;
I could make each arm a branch.

Let me begin as stem and leaf.
I'll make something you can breathe.

Gifted

That woman, she said, could rattle a bird
right out of the sky; that man
could spell a row of corn backwards
and forwards. Their children (all ten of them)
could tell you how to add leaf to branch
or divide the sky cloud by cloud.
They were a talented family,
a most gifted group.

And when they wanted a vacation,
they painted a wall full of mountains
and climbed the highest one,
they carved a coastline along the sidewalk
so that they could gaze out to sea
beyond the garage's shore.

They could sing harmony to a song
that was only, just then, being composed.
They believed in things that no one—not
even God—would have asked them to believe.
They knew how to keep stars
shining and they still do.

Coming Back to the Body

Coming back to the body, as if to
a house abandoned in time of war, you find
it stands as tall as you left it, the same
fingers reaching back to rub the same neck.

Returning, you remember how it feels
to stretch your arms to embrace another
body, how the tongue clicks against the teeth,
how solid voices flow into your ear.

You are relieved that what you dreamed will not
come true now that you have escaped again
into skin and bone. They'll never think of
looking for you in the body, alive.

Wherever the body is, that's where you
are now. It's the same old address you had
before you went away: no miracles,
no amazing improvements. You're still you.

Now that you are back, things go on the way
they were meant to. No one asks the question
that you couldn't answer if you wanted:
Where were you hiding all those long lost years?

Seeing off the Dead

We are all dying to know what is going
to happen when we're dead. Even if we pretend
we're not, we are. Just look at all of us

Growing older. Not one turning back
in her bones, not one hair going from gray
to black by itself. The body seems bent

On decline. The brain gradually loses
interest in the things of this world.
We've all seen the truly ancient ones,

Waiting in their chairs at the last train stop.
The conductor is nodding to them, and
they are allowed to go on, beyond the station.

They salute us with their lucky tickets.
They look so happy to be on their way;
we almost grow younger just watching them.

Into Thin Air

The expense of spirit is, in fact, what
I worry about. Not so much the body,
dragging itself from limb to limb,
falling helplessly down the vast
recesses of night, hanging between
dream and the uneven ticking of clocks.

Not so much even the eyes failing, light
spent, especially when I consider Degas,
who had the weakest eyes in Paris,
still managed to draw a black line around
the body, shoulders edged with a perfection
no one else, seeing better, could ever find.

But who is it, I wonder, who also serves?
And what is it to only stand and wait?
O body swayed and brightening glance,
cast off that waste of shame, and think
(beating mind!) of how it will be to fade
into thin air! What expense of spirit!

The Assumption

That would be the way to go:
straight up on a cloud,
the crowd below craning
their necks as you disappeared
out of view and then
the wondering: which cloud
overhead was under you.

There would be no dying then
for you; you would be one of
the seldom few, who did not need
to disembark but kept her place
as the boat went over the waterfall,
as the camel passed through
the eye of the needle,

as the soldiers searched the train.
And what made you so lucky? What
had you ever done to deserve this
favor? Nothing, not one thing. No
immaculate conception, no swing
low sweet chariot, no friendship with
an angel. You just assumed that it

would happen this way, that
all the practice shots, the dress
rehearsals, the final countdown,
none of it mattered. You assumed
that you would be lifted up, up, and
away—and you were, oh yes, you were.

JOYCE SUTPHEN grew up on a farm near St. Joseph, Minnesota, in Stearns County. After twelve years of Catholic schools, she attended the University of Minnesota in the late 60s, where she studied literature. Then, like many of the people she had read about, she set out on a long journey to find truth and beauty. As usual, the road led straight back to the beginning: home, country roads, the sun setting through the woods.

Towards the end of the century she finished her doctorate in English Literature, won the Barnard New Women Poets Prize, and her first book, *Straight Out of View*, was published by Beacon Press (1995). Her poems have appeared in *Poetry, American Poetry Review, Atlanta Review, Minnesota Monthly, North Dakota Review*, and many other journals, and she was a guest on *A Prairie Home Companion*, hosted by Garrison Keillor. Awards include a Minnesota State Arts Board Fellowship for poetry in 1998, two Jerome Foundation Awards, the Eunice Tietjens Memorial Prize, and a Minnesota State Arts Board Career Opportunity Grant.

She teaches Literature and Creative Writing at Gustavus Adolphus College in St. Peter, Minnesota. Her three daughters, Sarah, Alicia, and Marna, are grown up, and they all live in the Minneapolis-St. Paul area, which makes their mother very happy. Her parents, Robert and Rita Rassier, are keeping the farm as beautiful as it always was.

Acknowledgements

"Doppler Effect," *Aggassiz Review,* Fall, 1993.

"The Temptation to Invent," *Poetry,* February, 1995.

"Resurrection #6," *Poetry,* February, 1996.

"Of Virtue," *Poetry,* February, 1996.

"Not For Burning," *Poetry,* February, 1996.

"Not For Burning," and "Of Virtue," *1995/1996 Anthology of Magazine Verse &
Yearbook of American Poetry*, Ed. Alan Pater.

"Condition," *Poetry,* February, 1996.

"A Kind of Villanelle," *Artword Quarterly,* Summer, 1996.

"Bookmobile," *Atlanta Review,* Fall, 1996.

"The Fields in Late October," *Minnesota Monthly*, October, 1996.

"Fieldwork," *North Coast Review,* Fall/Winter, 1997.

"The Exorcism," *American Poetry Review*, March-April, 1997.

"Wanted" and "Late in the Century," *Sidewalks,* Fall/Winter, 1997-98.

"Her Legendary Head," *Poetry,* June, 1998.

"Sometimes Never," *Poetry,* August, 1998.

"Possibilities," *Minnesota English Journal,* Fall, 1998.

"A Way to Survive," *Minnesota English Journal,* Fall, 1998.

"Bell Bottom Dream," *Visions International*, 1998.

"Casino," *Atlantic Review,* Fall/Winter, 1998 (International Poetry
Competition issue).

"Gifted," *Twin Cities Revue*, January, 1999.

"The Silence Says," *Minnesota Monthly,* April, 1999.

"The Haircut," *Rag Mag,* Spring, 1999.

"The Rosary of the World," *ArtWord Quarterly,* Spring, 1999.

"Arrangement in Grey and Black," *Sidewalks*, Spring/Summer, 1999.

"Into Thin Air," *Poetry*, July, 1999.

"Natural Selection," 2000 *Minnesota Poetry Calendar*.

"The Shop," *ArtWord Quarterly,* Winter, 2000.

"Semi-Literate" appeared on *Poetry Daily* (www.poems.com) in April, 1999.

"Here is My Father," "Apple Season," and "Kingdom of Summer" were
broadcast on *A Prairie Home Companion*, October 24, 1998 (Minnesota
Public Radio).

"Here is My Father," "Girl on a Tractor," *North Dakota Review*.

"The Assumption," *Minnesota Monthly,* September, 1999.

"Seeing Off the Dead," "Night and Day," *Poetry,* September, 1999.

"The Problem Was," *Poetry,* February, 2000.

"Homesteading," *Poetry,* April, 2000.

"Homesteading" appeared on *Poetry Daily* (www.poems.com) in April, 2000.

"Acoustic Alibi," *The Bloomsbury Review,* May/June, 2000.

"Chagall's Lovers," *North Coast Review,* Summer, 2000.

"What the Heart Cannot Forget," and "After Magritte," *Luna,* 2000.